D1601962

WITHDRAWN ORINDA

PASSOVER
AS I REMEMBER IT

written by Toby Knobel Fluek
with Lillian Fluek Finkler

Illustrated by Toby Knobel Fluek

CONTRA COSTA COUNTY LIBRARY

ALFRED A. KNOPF   NEW YORK

3 1901 01783 9863

We dedicate this book to our family —
Max, Steve, David, and Gary —
for the happy Passovers we celebrate together

THIS IS A BORZOI BOOK PUBLISHED BY ALFRED A. KNOPF, INC.

Text copyright © 1994 by Toby Knobel Fluek & Lillian Fluek Finkler
Illustrations © 1994 by Toby Knobel Fluek
All rights reserved under International and Pan-American Copyright Conventions.
Published in the United States of America by Alfred A. Knopf, Inc., New York, and simultaneously in Canada
by Random House of Canada Limited, Toronto. Distributed by Random House, Inc., New York.

Manufactured in the United States of America
Book design by Mina Greenstein
1 3 5 7 9 10 8 6 4 2

Library of Congress Cataloging-in-Publication Data
Fluek, Toby Knobel.
Passover as I remember it / written by Toby Knobel Fluek and Lillian Fluek Finkler ;
illustrated by Toby Knobel Fluek.
p. cm.
Summary: The author describes how her family prepared for and celebrated Passover in the years before
World War II while living in Czernica, a small village located at that time in Poland.
ISBN 0-679-83876-7 (trade)
1. Fluek, Toby Knobel—Juvenile literature. 2. Jews—Ukraine—Chernitsa (L'vovskaia oblast')—
Biography—Juvenile literature. 3. Chernitsa (L'vovskaia oblast', Ukraine)—Biography—Juvenile literature.
4. Jews—Ukraine—Chernitsa (L'vovskaia oblast')—Social life and customs—Juvenile literature.
5. Passover—Customs and practices—Juvenile literature. 6. Passover in art—Juvenile literature.
[1. Passover. 2. Jews—Poland—Social life and customs.] I. Finkler, Lillian Fluek, ill. II. Title.
DS135.P63F6 1994 947'.718—dc20 92-9020

Jews all over the world celebrate Passover, the holiday of freedom, the holiday of spring. The food and customs vary in different countries, but the ritual is the same.

In this book, I tell of a life that no longer exists in Poland. A few years after this Passover of my childhood, World War II began, and my father, my two sisters, my brother, and most of the Jews of Czernica—and of Europe—perished at the hands of Hitler and the Nazis. With them, a tradition and a way of life found only in these rural villages was destroyed. In our family, only my mother and I survived the Holocaust. Very few Jews are left in Poland now, and most of those who remain live in cities.

I now celebrate Passover in the United States with my husband, Max, my daughter, Lillian, and her husband, Steve, and my two grandsons, David and Gary. Although modern conveniences make getting ready for Passover easier than it used to be, we prepare and clean for the holiday as we used to in my old home, and I follow many of the customs of my childhood.

My husband still chants the Haggadah in Hebrew, as his father did, but for the Seder with our children and grandchildren, we combine, reading the Haggadah and singing the songs in both Hebrew and English. We sing the songs with new melodies that we have learned in this country, and like many other Americans, we now hide the *afikomen* for the children to find.

Toby on the Farm

When I was a little girl, I lived in Czernica, a small village in Poland. I lived with my two older sisters, Surcie and Lajcie, my older brother, Aron, and my parents.

We were a close-knit family; there was warmth and caring for one another among our relatives and neighbors. We were one of only ten Jewish families among 250 Gentile families. We got along well with the Polish and Ukrainian neighbors, although once in a while we heard some anti-Semitic remarks.

In our village, there was no electricity. We used kerosene lamps. We had no running water in the house. Water was brought in by the bucketful from the shallow wells along the river. We cooked on a woodburning stove and baked our own bread. Our house had earthen floors.

We lived a simple life. My only toy was a doll, which my sister Lajcie made for me from rags. I was always lonely, because I was the only young Jewish child in the village, and my parents didn't allow me to play with the local children. Mother wanted to shield me from being teased because I was Jewish. I attended the Polish school, and that was the only place where I mingled with other children.

My parents made a living farming and *hondeling*, or trading, and they were always short of money. But for the Sabbath—*Shabbes*—and holidays, they saved every penny they could.

My favorite holiday was Passover. That was the time I got new shoes and sometimes a new dress, and we ate meat every day for a whole week.

Making Goose Fat

In December, after Chanukah, Mother began to prepare the goose fat for Passover. We kept geese in a cage, and Mother stuffed them with dough and special grains until they were fat. She took the geese to the slaughterer in Podkamien, a nearby *shtetl*, or small town. The goose fat was cooked and then stored in a cold place on top of the foyer closet. The *greeven*, fried pieces of leftover fatty skin, we enjoyed right away, eating it plain on bread or at dinner with black radishes or bow-tie noodles and *pirogen*—dumplings. Eating *greeven* reminded me of the delicious Passover food, and I couldn't wait for the holiday to come.

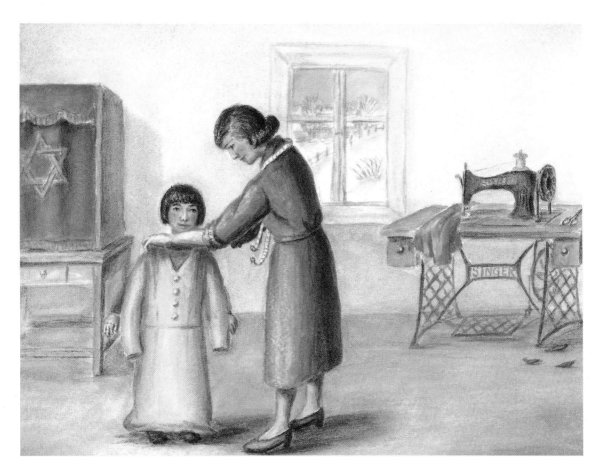

Dressmaker

In the middle of January, before my sister Surcie, who was a dressmaker, got busy with her holiday sewing for the neighbors, she made dresses for our family. She would resew old clothes that my aunt Sarah had sent from America. If the color of the dress was faded from wear, my sister *nitzevit*—turned—it. She took it completely apart, recut it to my size, resewed it inside out—and that is how I got my new dress.

Shoemaker

I was very excited when my mother told me in March that it was time to have my new shoes made for Passover. Mother bought leather from Hersh Milrom, a merchant, and we took it to Ivan, the village shoemaker. First he measured my foot. Then he cut the leather, glued it, sewed it, and knocked the shoe together with little wooden pegs called *fleklach*. It took him a whole week to make my new pair of shoes. During the year, many people had their shoes *latted*, or patched, but for the holidays they would get new shoes.

Gathering Eggs

We owned twelve chickens, and in the early spring, they started laying eggs. It was my job to collect them. Each hen made her own nest in the hay and would lay her eggs there every time. I would climb up the stepladder to find the nests in the hay. I walked quietly so I wouldn't scare the hens, and I put the eggs into my basket gently so they wouldn't break. We stored the eggs in a wooden box in the pantry. Mother used about 200 eggs during Passover.

Making Wine

Five weeks before Passover, Mother made the wine. I helped cut the raisins, even though she would scold me for *noshing*—snacking—on too many of them. Mother put the raisins into a large glass bottle with sugar and water. She covered it with a thin cloth and put it on top of the closet near the stove. When the mixture had fermented and tasted just right, Mother squeezed it through a cheese-cloth. I liked to watch her, but I wasn't allowed to sample the wine before the Seder. The wine actually tasted like raisin juice, but we didn't know any better and enjoyed it just the same.

Making Borscht

One of my favorite Passover dishes was borscht, a beet soup. Mother would peel and cut up several basketfuls of beets from our garden and put them in water in a covered barrel. After four weeks, the beets had soured, and mildew had settled on top. Mother cleaned off the mildew and cooked a delicious borscht from the sour beets.

While Mother got ready for the holidays, Father worked around the farm, cleaning the stable and getting the grain ready for spring planting. Every day, Father and Lajcie would prepare food for our animals by mixing cut straw with chopped potatoes or potato peels.

Spring Cleaning

Three weeks before Passover, Mother hired Katerina, our neighbor, to do the laundry. In return, Surcie sewed blouses for her. In a *balia*, a wooden washtub, Katerina scrubbed our linen sheets, towels, feather-bed covers, and Father's shirts. She boiled the laundry and rinsed it in the river, beating it with a wooden board. It took her two days to do it all. Afterward, she whitewashed the walls in the large room and kitchen, using a brush made from cornstalks.

Meanwhile, Father put fresh straw into the linen sacks that were our mattresses. To make the dirt floors look clean, Lajcie painted them with yellow mud that we dug up from the backyard.

Giving Charity

Every family, rich or poor, conducted their own Seder. Only a homeless Jewish person would be invited to a Seder. Instead, it was customary to give the poor money to buy food, so they could make a Seder in their own home.

Before Passover, my father gave *maos chittin*, which means "wheat money," to the Rabbi in Podkamien. My parents also helped my uncle Mordche and his family, giving them meat and vegetables from our garden for their Seder. He was my favorite uncle, a poor man struggling to make a living, and I was happy that we could help him.

Flour for Matzos

Father took special care to make the Passover flour for baking our matzos. The previous fall, he supervised the harvesting of the wheat, as required by Orthodox law. He made sure it didn't get wet from the rain before it was brought to the barn to be stored. During the winter, the mill would be made kosher—*kashered*—by cleaning it thoroughly under a rabbi's supervision. Only then was the special wheat ground into flour. Two weeks before Passover, we baked our own matzos. Mother invited our neighbors to bake their matzos in our home, and it became a community project.

Baking Matzos

I loved the excitement when our Jewish neighbors crowded into our large room to bake matzos. They brought sacks of flour and rolling pins, and wore clean aprons, with scarves covering their hair. As my sister Surcie mixed the flour in a brass basin, I added water. She kneaded it quickly, then Mother rolled out the dough, and I made the holes. All the women kneaded and rolled at once, then Father put the matzos into the oven. The mixing, kneading, and rolling had to be completed in less than eighteen minutes so that the dough would not have time to rise. My parents baked forty pounds of matzos for our family. The matzos were hung from the attic ceiling in a feather-bed cover, away from any *chometz*—leavened bread and other non-Passover food.

More Cleaning

The week before Passover, we aired out our clothing and the feather beds and pillows. To remove the dust, Lajcie would beat them with a *tchepatchke*, a wicker utensil, and would cover them with fancy damask linens. Then she scrubbed the wooden benches. Mother carried the baking utensils to the river and washed out the dough particles, because the house had to be *completely* free of leavened bread for Passover. I liked to clean the drawers and shelves and keep the linen closet neat, but I didn't like scrubbing the mud off and polishing the shoes for our whole family. Meanwhile, Surcie was finishing the sewing she had promised people for the holidays.

The Slaughterer

During the year, we ate meat only at *Shabbes* meals. Mother would go to Podkamien to have the chicken slaughtered. Two days before Passover, Father brought the *shochet*—the ritual slaughterer—by horse and buggy to our farm. All the Jewish women in our village came to our backyard with their chickens. Although I felt sorry for the chickens, I still liked eating chicken soup and drumsticks. Father also had a calf slaughtered to sell additional meat to the Jewish families. We ate meat every day during the eight days of Passover, and I couldn't wait for the holiday to start.

Searching for Chometz

The night before the first Seder, we performed a ritual called *boy-dek chometz*—the search for the bread. Mother held a lit candle, and Father carried a goose feather and a wooden spoon. We walked from window to window looking for pieces of bread that Father had placed there earlier. Father recited a benediction while he brushed the bread and crumbs from each window. The next morning, the wooden spoon, feather, and bread were burned in a special fire in the stove.

Another ritual was the selling of the *chometz*. A week earlier, Father had given a donation to the Rabbi and told him of all the *chometz* we had at home and on our farm. The Rabbi sold it symbolically to a non-Jew, which meant that we didn't own any *chometz* during Passover, fulfilling the commandment.

Unpacking the Passover Dishes

That same evening, Mother brought down the Passover dishes from the attic. I smacked my lips when I saw the brown glazed pots in which she baked *keeslach*—a kind of pudding—from boiled potatoes and eggs. As she unpacked each pot and pan, she told me who gave it to her. Grandma Chaje-Dine gave the bowl with the red flower design, and the white enamel pot came from Aunt Matel. Then she unpacked the Elijah cup and a glass wine cup for everyone in our family. Mine was the smallest, with a little handle. Father had a silver *becher*, a Kiddush cup.

Kashering Silverware

We didn't have separate Passover silverware, so my parents *kashered* the spoons, forks, and knives we used every day. A day before the Seder, Father put them in a hole in our backyard. He brought out a stone that had been heated until it was red-hot and placed it in the hole. Mother poured in a potful of heated water. The hot stone brought the water to a boil, and that made the utensils kosher for Passover. I was fascinated by this.

The same day, Mother *kashered* the woodburning stove by painting it with whitewash and heating it until the top iron sheet became a fiery red.

Cooking

After breakfast, on the morning of the Seder, the last crumbs of bread were burned. Mother cleaned the kitchen again, and Father brought in a large Passover kitchen tabletop. Then Mother started preparing the food for the Seder.

I stood at the table, imagining potato pancakes fried in oil, until Mother put me to work peeling potatoes. Mother cooked gefilte fish, chicken, flanken, and *tzimmes*—carrots with chicken fat. She made noodles from eggs and potato starch, and dessert from dried apples. For lunch, we ate a mixture of boiled potatoes, goose fat, onions, and boiled eggs with borscht. We weren't allowed to taste anything else. We could only smell the aromas and wait for the Seder.

Making Charoses

After lunch, while Mother cooked and Surcie ironed our holiday dresses, Father prepared the *charoses*, which represented the mortar—cement—made by Hebrew slaves in Egypt. We had picked the nuts from the walnut tree last summer. I remembered peeling off the green hulls and drying the nuts in the hot sun.

Father crushed the nuts with a mortar and pestle, which had been in our family for generations. He added chopped apples, wine, and cinnamon. I wasn't allowed to taste the *charoses* before the Seder, but I could wait, for I knew it would be starting soon.

The Seder Plate

Father made up the Seder plate, which holds the symbols of the Passover story. A *gargele*, or chicken neck, was the roasted shank bone, which represents the Passover offering. Father also roasted a hard-boiled egg, another symbol of the Passover offering. He cut pieces of horseradish from our garden for the *maror*, the bitter herbs, which stood for the bitterness of our people in slavery. I would run from the room, because the smell of the horseradish burned my eyes. There was a piece of boiled potato—*karpas*—for each of us, representing spring. All this, with the *charoses*, was placed on the table next to the matzo.

Setting the Table

Toward evening, Surcie and Father carried the table over to the bed, where he would conduct the Seder. Mother blessed the candles, which were set in brass candlesticks, a wedding gift from her mother. Dressed in a *kapote*—a long black holiday coat—Father lay down on the feather bed, leaning back on pillows. He would eat lying down, a symbol—dating from ancient times—that he was a free man. We sat on a bench facing Father. The table was covered with a white damask tablecloth and set with the wine cups and wine, the Elijah cup, three matzos in a very old embroidered matzo cover, the Seder plate, and a dish of salt water. I admired the festive table.

The Seder

My father poured the first cup of wine for each of us, then he filled the Elijah cup with wine and made Kiddush, reciting the blessing over the wine. We all repeated the blessing and drank the first cup. Mother brought water to the bedside, and Father poured it over his hands into a brass basin. Then each of us took a piece of potato and dipped it in the salt water, to remind us of our sweat and tears when we were slaves in Egypt.

Next Father took the middle matzo from under the matzo cover, broke it in half, and placed one half, the *afikomen*—literally "dessert"— under the tablecloth.

The Four Questions

Father refilled the wine cups, and my brother, as the youngest boy present, asked the four questions in Yiddish. Why is this night different from all other nights?

Why do we eat matzo instead of bread?

Why do we eat bitter herbs?

Why do we dip our foods two times?

Why do we eat lying down?

My father chanted the first sentence in Yiddish, *"Knecht zennen mir geveysen"*—we were slaves—and continued in Hebrew, reading the Passover story in the Haggadah, as his father had done. The girls didn't have Haggadahs, and I didn't understand Hebrew, so I listened to the monotone melody and remembered the stories my mother had told me while she cooked for the Seder.

The Passover Story

Mother had explained that Passover is the holiday of deliverance for the Jewish people. In the days of the Bible, the Hebrews went to Egypt because there was no food in their land of Canaan, now known as Israel. Pharaoh, the Egyptian king, grew afraid of the Hebrews and turned them into slaves. The Hebrews had to work making bricks and building pyramids. God told Moses to tell Pharaoh: "Let my people go." Pharaoh refused, and God punished the Egyptians with ten plagues, so Pharaoh would change his mind. God made the river water turn bloody red and sent frogs to the land. Locusts ate the wheat, the cattle became diseased, and other terrible things happened. For the last plague, all the first-born Egyptian sons died, including Pharaoh's own son. But God passed over the Hebrews' homes, and their sons lived. And this is where the name of the holiday—*Pesach* in Hebrew—comes from.

Flight from Egypt

We repeated the ten plagues with Father, using our pinkies to remove a drop of wine for each of the plagues, because we shouldn't be happy with a full cup while the Egyptians, also God's children, perished.

After the plagues, Pharaoh freed the Hebrews. They left Egypt so quickly they had no time to let their bread rise. They rolled out the dough, and the hot sun baked it as they hurried away. It was good that they left quickly, because Pharaoh changed his mind and sent his army after the Hebrews. God parted the Red Sea waters for the fleeing Hebrews, but the Egyptians, in pursuit, drowned in the sea.

Father washed his hands after saying the blessing and drinking the second cup of wine. It was time to eat the matzo, to remember that God took us out of Egypt to freedom. Next we dipped the bitter herbs into the sweet *charoses*. I made sure to chew only the tiniest piece of horseradish. Finally, the delicious Seder meal could begin.

Elijah

After the meal, Father gave everyone a piece of the *afikomen* and continued to chant the Haggadah in the traditional tune, thanking God for the miracles of the Passover holiday. I fell asleep at the table, while my father and brother continued reading the Haggadah well into the night. Mother woke me for the third cup of wine, and to open the door for *Eliyahu HaNovie*, Elijah the Prophet. We believed he would visit all Jewish homes, bringing the good news of the coming redemption of Israel and a great age of peace. His cup stood on the table, filled with wine. After opening the door, I ran to see if any wine was missing from the cup. My brother, Aron, shook the table and teased me, saying, "Look, Elijah is drinking the wine." After drinking the fourth cup of wine, we finished the Seder by reciting *"Leshanah haba'ah biYerushala'yim"*—next year in Jerusalem.

The Second Night

At the second night's Seder, Father again chanted the entire Haggadah. We finished the *charoses* and the symbolic burned egg from the Seder plate, and ate another delicious Seder meal. Afterward, Mother saved a piece of the *afikomen* for next year, believing that this brought good luck.

Chol Hamoed, the middle days of Passover, was a festive time. In the *shtetl*, many people didn't work at all, because the whole week was considered a holiday. Even in our small village, we would *shpatzir*—stroll the streets—and I liked to show off my new dress and shoes. It was known as the time to get engaged, and brides and grooms would visit each other's families.

Making Matzo Meal

Some people ate matzo meal for the whole eight days of Passover. My father was a very religious man who believed that it was not proper to eat matzo meal until the end of Passover. We waited until the last day of Passover, and that's when we ate matzo balls and matzo meal *latkes*, or pancakes.

During *Chol Hamoed*, my sister Lajcie made matzo meal by crushing broken matzos in a wooden stamper, fashioned from a hollowed-out log. As we sat down to the last Passover dinner, I thought that I would miss the holiday meals. Still, I looked forward to fresh bread.

The End of Passover

Passover ended too quickly for me. I enjoyed the preparation, the festivities, the Seder, and the delicious food. I felt sad when my mother packed up the dishes, but she was relieved that she wouldn't have to cook so much.

Now that spring was here, Father would have the fields plowed. He would plant potatoes and sow the grain. Mother was ready to plant vegetables in the garden, and I knew that the school year would be coming to an end soon.

Mother took the dishes up to the attic and made a wish: "We should live until next year to celebrate Passover again in good health."